David W. Menard

USAF
PLUS FIFTEEN

A Photo History
1947-1962

Schiffer Military/Aviation History
Atglen, PA

Dedication
This book is dedicated to all pilots, crews, and aircraft maintainers past, present and future.

Book Design by Robert Biondi

First Edition
Copyright © 1993 by David W. Menard.
Library of Congress Catalog Number: 92-63123

Printed in the United States of America.
ISBN: 0-88740-483-9

We are interested in hearing from authors with book ideas on related topics.

Published by Schiffer Publishing Ltd.
77 Lower Valley Road
Atglen, PA 19310
Please write for a free catalog.
This book may be purchased from the publisher.
Please include $2.95 postage.
Try your bookstore first.

Introduction

History notes that the U.S. Air Force became an independent service on September 17, 1947. During the next fifteen years, the Air Force transitioned from propellers to jet propulsion, brown uniforms to blue, subsonic speeds to Mach Two, fought a "police action" and defended most of the Free World. The variety of aircraft types, missions, and markings during this era will never be seen again. Left over World War II fabric covered gliders assigned to rescue squadrons could be parked next to the latest jet fighter or bomber. Colorful unit markings on the combat types were the rule, not the exception. Some people might then ask why there isn't more photographic coverage of this era. It was one of the peak periods of the Cold War, and photo taking was considered a breach of security, perhaps not so much the main subject but what might be in the background. Even such innocent examples as overall orange target tug T-33s or C-45s with SAC crest and "Milky Way" were off limits. Paranoia reigned, and some were more paranoid than others, i.e., how many photos of operationally marked SAC B-47s have been published? But many personnel carried and used cameras anyway, managing to record much of this variety for future historians, modelers, and enthusiasts. So for over 30 years, contacts with many of these amateur photographers have led to an interesting collection of slides. This volume is composed mostly of these shots. All were taken between late 1947 and late 1962, and very few are from official sources. Several of the more colorful examples are shown with two views to better illustrate some of the more interesting types.

The designations used in the captions are those in use at the time of the photo, and should not be confused with ones used later. For instance, prior to 15 August 1955, the E prefix stood for Exempt, not Electronic. The prefix A on a transport such as a C-47 or C-54 prior to 1962 meant the aircraft was used to check landing and navigational aids, not as attack gunships. An MC-54 or MC-131A was a medical evacuation version, not a special operations one. The S prefix was for search and rescue.

The reader might notice that there are more fighters in this compilation. Two reasons for that: they generally carried the flashiest markings, and more of their pilots and maintenance personnel took slides and shared their material. But the bright yellows carried by the rescue aircraft catch one's eye also, indicating aircraft flown by some of the bravest crews of all. Transports might have been slow and ungainly, but they delivered the goods when required, so they are not forgotten in this book.

So please enjoy this collection of photos and try to place yourself mentally back in those exciting days of USAF Plus Fifteen.

USAF PLUS FIFTEEN

One of the 49th Fighter Squadron's new F-84Bs is examined by unit personnel, while a soon to be replaced F-47N sits in the background. (Mr. Luscombe)

This brand new P-84B carries freshly painted insignia red arctic markings prior to her flight to Ladd AFB, AK for cold weather testing. (F. Stroud)

Colonel Dave Shilling's P-80A carried his World War II score at the National Air Races in September 1947. (W.J. Balogh, Sr.)

Lined up for review are these F-82Es of the 8th Air Forces' 27th Fighter Wing. (R. Williams/W. Thompson)

The only unit to fly the F-82E was SAC's 27th Fighter Wing from Kearney Field, NE. (R. Williams/W. Thompson)

27th Fighter Wing F-82Es show off their formation flying. (Lt.Colonel B. Mitchell)

The Tenn. ANG flew the F-47D in the late 1940s with unusual (for a Guard unit) markings on their tails. (C. Graham)

Another Tenn. ANG F-47D displays its unique markings (C. Graham)

The 37th Fighter Squadron flew these yellow and black F-84Bs at Dow AFB, Maine. (W.J. Balogh, Sr.)

These McDonnell employees are getting one of the XF-85s ready for a ground engine run. (USAF)

The bleak and desolate location of Davis AFB, AK shows well behind the B-26C. (via M. Isham)

The third F-80 unit to serve in Europe was the 36th Fighter Wing starting in 1948, and this B model carries 23rd FBS colors. (R. Kamm)

Crew members of this C-82A use it for "box seats" at the 1948 National Air Races. (W.J. Balogh, Sr.)

Left and below: The 4th Rescue Squadron flew this beautiful SA-10A from Hamilton AFB, CA. (W.T. Larkins)

Cruising high over Hawaii is an F-47N of the 81st Fighter Wing just prior to the unit's move to Kirtland AFB, NM. (Lt. Colonel R. Satterfield)

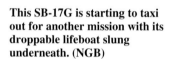

This SB-17G is starting to taxi out for another mission with its droppable lifeboat slung underneath. (NGB)

Yellow trim on this F-84C indicated assignment to the 59th Fighter Squadron at Otis AFB, MA. (Lt.Colonel W. Greenlalgh)

This F-84C is from the 58th Fighter Squadron of the 33rd Fighter Group. (Lt.Colonel W. Greenlalgh)

The first unit to fly the F-84C was the 33rd Fighter Group at Walker, AFB, NM. (Lt.Colonel W. Greenlalgh)

Sporting eye-catching insignia red arctic markings, this 7th Bomb Group B-36B revs up her engines prior to take-off. (USAF)

The second B-45C built is leaving a large exhaust trail during take-off from Muroc AFB, CA. (USAF)

This F-80A carries one of the better known squadron insignias in AF history, the 334th Fighter Squadron rooster with boxing gloves. (W.T. Larkins)

One of the last Black Widows in the AF was this Far East Air Forces F-61C photographed at Misawa AB, Japan. (M. Zeljak)

Some of the flight crew walk out of their B-36B parked at Carswell AFB, TX. (Lt.Colonel C. Toynbee)

The Sunrise Mountains loom in the background of these F-80As based at Nellis AFB, NV. (USAF)

One of the B-26Bs used by the 86th Fighter Wing in Germany as a target tug had a face on its nose. (Colonel C. Horton)

The 52nd Fighter Group F-82Fs carried the flashiest color scheme of any Twin Mustang unit. (W.T. Larkins)

F-80Cs began to arrive in Japan in late 1949; this one was assigned to the 41st Fighter Squadron at Johnson AB, Japan. (M. Zeljak)

The Commander of the 20th Fighter Wing at Shaw AFB, SC flew this F-84B. (USAF)

The other wing to receive the F-84B was the 20th at Shaw AFB, where this 77th Fighter Squadron example was photographed. (USAF)

Below zero weather was just one of the hazards that Alaska based H-5Gs of the 10th Rescue Squadron had to contend with. (USAF)

The Delaware ANG's first fighters were the long range F-47N. (Lt.Colonel E. Bosetti)

The first American delta winged jet, the XF-92A, basks in the San Diego sunshine. (USAF)

An Alaskan based SC-47D cruises over the Brooks Range. (USAF)

Many Troop Carrier C-82As carried insignia red arctic markings such as this one. (E. Van Houten)

The World War II style tail markings on B-29s lasted until after the Korean War, such as this arrow in the circle for the 509th Bomb Group. (E. Van Houten)

Right and below: The Alaska based 10th Rescue Squadron had this beautiful LC-126A assigned to it. (Colonel H.B. Allen)

The bleakness of Davis AFB, AK did not deter the Airways and Air Communications Service (AACS) from their duties with this C-47D. (via M. Isham)

This C-54G displays her Berlin Airlift fleet number on her tail in very large digits. (Colonel J.J. Tarsitano)

The 31st Fighter Wing was based at Turner AFB, GA with F-84Cs such as this one. (Ed. Galbraith)

Checkered nosed F-84Cs meant the aircraft were assigned to the 31st Fighter Wing. (Lt.Colonel C. Toynbee)

The 332nd Fighter Group flew F-47Ns when based at Lockbourne AFB, Ohio. (W.T. Larkins)

This F-51D is assigned to the commander of Williams AFB, AZ, Colonel Robert L. Scott. (NG Bureau)

The only B-26 to have a J31 engine installed in its tail was this XB-26F. (W.T. Larkins)

Melting snow at Misawa AB, Japan will make the ground crews work on these F-82Gs, SB-17Gs, and B-29 a bit easier. (R. Esposito Collection)

A visiting H-5G taxis on the Nellis AFB, NV ramp. (NGB)

Misawa AB, Japan had three F-80A squadrons assigned in 1949, and this F-80A was assigned to one of them, the 9th. (A. Coleman)

Here is an F-80A of the 8th Fighter Squadron at Misawa AB, Japan. (M. Zeljak)

The yellow and black checkerboard on the tail of this T-28A indicated its assignment to Nellis AFB, NV. (NGB)

Left and below: The 2nd Rescue Squadron on Okinawa acquired an ex-305th Bomb Group B-17G with all its armament removed for duty in the rescue mission and then painted all required markings themselves. (A.W. George)

Sporting unblemished arctic markings, this B-45A was photographed en route to Ladd AFB, AK from Wright Field. (Unknown)

Multiple color banding usually means a commanders' aircraft, such as this F-80C of the 8th FBW in the spring of 1950. (DeWald)

The 2nd Rescue Squadron on Okinawa used this H-6A. (A.W. George)

This brand new TF-80C is as shiny as a new penny. (E. Van Houten)

The exact reason for the A suffix to the radio call number on this VB-17G is unknown, but possibly it meant the aircraft was assigned to an Army general. (R. Hubbard)

Elmendorf AFB's 57th Fighter Group sent a flight of F-80Cs to a gunnery meet at Nellis AFB in spring 1950, and this one is the Groups Commander's. (W.T. Larkins)

When SAC first started using their star spangled band, such as on this B-26B, it did not take the troops long to call it the "Milky Way." (W.T. Larkins)

The extreme cold and wind at Goose AB, Labrador has helped chip off the blue paint from this SA-10A. (E. Van Houten)

This 4th F(AW) Squadron F-82G is nicknamed "Call Girl" and was based at Naha AB, Okinawa. (J. Spry)

The second TF-80C (later redesignated T-33A) was used as an ejection seat test aircraft at both Wright and Edwards AFBs as a ETF-80C. (USAF)

A MATS C-74 is shown parked next to a SAC C-54. (D. Watt)

The yellow color of this H-5G assigned to a rescue unit at Goose AB contrasts well with the snow. (E. Van Houghton)

The 1st Rescue Squadron flew this SC-47D. (USAF)

Some fledgling mechanics are shown here learning to start a 335th FS F-80A. (USAF)

Five F-80Cs of the 41st FBS from Johnson AB, Japan sit in the snow at Misawa AB. (Colonel J.S. Jenkins)

The first unit in Europe to receive the F-84E was the 36th FBW at Furstenfeldbruck AB, Germany. (USAF)

Caught near Mt. Fuji a few weeks before the start of the Korean War is the F-80C of the 35th FBS that is on display today in the USAF Museum. (H. Boyce)

This SB-17G based on Okinawa finished its career at Clark, AB, RP with an overall black paint scheme. (A.W. George)

The commander of the 31st Fighter Wing flew this F-84E. (Lt.Colonel C. Toynbee)

A unique aircraft to be based at Goose AB, Newfoundland was this CG-15A complete with a cabin heater mounted on its top. (E. Van Houten)

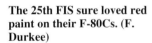

The 25th FIS sure loved red paint on their F-80Cs. (F. Durkee)

These tanks are being loaded into a C-124A of the 2nd Strategic Support Squadron. (USAF)

The 27th FEW F-84Es got to Korea aboard the USS Bataan, and here is one being hoisted aboard at NAS Alameda. (D. Watt)

A crew chief of the 2nd Fighter Interceptor Squadron services the fuselage tank on his F-94A. (Colonel R. Uppstrom)

The Walker AFB, NM based 2nd Strategic Support Squadron had this YC-97 assigned as well as larger C-124As. (E. Van Houten)

The first AF jet aerobatic team in the US was the "ACROJETS" based at Williams AFB, AZ. (E.W. Quandt)

The first production C-124As were assigned to SAC units, such as the 3rd Strategic Support Squadron. (E. Van Houten)

The Okinawa based 2nd Rescue Squadron flew L-5Bs as well as SC-47s and SB-17s. (A.W. George)

Red trim on the Korean based
F-51Ds meant the 67th Fighter
Bomber Squadron. (J. Ortega)

This Edwards AFB assigned B-
47B was photographed while
visiting the Grumman airport.
(Colonel Uppstrom)

The two GIs are basking in sun
in front of an L-5G, C-64A, and
SA-10A at Goose AB, Labrador.
(E. Van Houten)

Ground crews go over these RB-26Cs prior to their flight to Korea for duty with the 67th TAC Recon. Wing. (Colonel R. Spence)

Taxiing into a strong wind is an Air Proving Ground Command F-84E carrying two 12" Tiny Tims, eight 5' HVAR rockets, and JATO for a demonstration flight at the 1951 Detroit air show. (E.W. Quandt)

The 3rd Rescue Squadron in Japan flew one of two C-46Ds to ever serve in the rescue role. (J. Chessington)

Left and below: Showing the effect of hot sun and salt air on paint, this 2nd Rescue Squadron C-46D sits on alert on Okinawa. (A.W. George)

One of the classic views of the Mustang is this image of an F-51D over northern California. (W.T. Larkins)

These 27th Fighter Escort Wing F-84Gs carry temporary markings for air-to-air gunnery exercises in the fall of 1951. (Lt.Colonel J. Meierdierck)

Taxiing a C-124A required a crew member to protrude through the top hatch to watch wing tip clearances. (R. Hallan)

The first pure jet transport in the United States was the XC-123A, an assault glider fitted with four J-47 jet engines. (W.D. Shipp)

The summer heat on bases in Korea meant that aircraft such as this C-119B strained on take-off. (Major T. Ingrassia)

This SH-19A is equipped with floats which enabled it to be amphibious. (Mr. Fagen)

The Okinawa based 2nd Rescue Squadron flew SB-17Gs such as this one. (A.W. George)

This 86th Fighter Group target-tug Invader carried the same tail markings as the unit's F-84Es. (H. Pritchard)

Right and below: Whoever painted the Rescue Squadron markings on this L-5A either didn't understand the instructions, or just got carried away! (Unknown)

T-33As assigned to the Korea based fighter groups carried two "hot" .50 caliber machine guns, as well as the same markings as the F-86s. (Davis Collection)

The A suffix on this F-80C buzz number meant there was another 726 in the 8th Fighter Bomber Wing. (C. Hoggard)

Three F-80Cs of 8 FBS fly a very nice echelon formation in May 1951. (Colonel B. Butcher)

Who would have thought this Nellis based F-84E would have ended her career on display in the USAF Museum where she is today. (ANG Bureau)

This North East Air Command C-47D dug in her skis when landing on soft snow, thus causing her left engine to wrench off. (J.B. Chessington)

F-80As were flown in the training mission at Williams AFB from the late 1940s to the early-1950s. (Colonel R. Merritt)

This "Captivair" T-6D was used as a cockpit procedures trainer at Perrin AFB, TX. (Colonel R. Merritt)

The insignia on this F-94B is the one used by Air Proving Ground Command during the early 1950s. (E.W. Quandt)

Shark-mouthed F-51D in FEAF meant 12th Fighter Bomber Squadron. (M. Zeljak)

Left and below: Two views of an SB-17G assigned to Goose AB help show her markings well. (E. Van Houten)

Early model T-33A used the underslung, tear drop shaped tip tanks. (Colonel R. Merritt)

Another Far East Forces (FEAF) unit that flew F-82Gs was the 68th Fighter (All Weather) Squadron, Itazuke AB, Japan. (Davis Collection)

Colonel William H. Clark was the commander of the 18th Fighter Bomber Group in Korea and flew this F-51D. (Thompson/Davis)

The 61st FIS F-94Bs at Selfridge AFB, MI used a shark mouth for a unit marking. (Lt.Colonel W.K. Thomas)

The commander of the 192nd Fighter Squadron, NV ANG, flew this F-51D to Iceland in 1952 to begin an AF presence that exists to this day. (Conger Collection)

The 51st Rescue Squadron at Narsarssuaq AB, Greenland used SB-17Gs and SC-47s to perform their mission. (D.R. Finders)

Since both the pilot and the crew chief of this 8th FBS F-84E were from Indiana, what better name for her but "Hoosier Hotshot." (Colonel D. James)

Polka-dotted spinners, and wing tips were the markings used by the 45th Tactical Recon Squadron RF-51Ds. (MGen. S. Newman)

The 55th Air Rescue Squadron at Thule AB, Greenland used many types of aircraft, including this SH-19A. (USAF)

The 47th Bomb Wing flew all of its B-45As from Langley AFB to RAF Sculthorpe in England during July 1952 to reinforce NATO. (USAF)

The second production T-28A was used by the Air Training Command, while the next several went to the Test Pilot School at Edwards. (Colonel R. Merritt)

This SH-21B has been temporarily assigned to the Wright Air Development Center at Wright Field. (W.J. Balogh, Sr.)

Air Training Command T-33As were rather plainly marked with the command badge and a buzz number on the nose. (Colonel R. Johnson)

Enid AFB, OK was home to this
blue trimmed B-25J. (W.T.
Larkins)

Right and below: Narsarssuaq
AB, Greenland was home
base for this ski equipped SC-
47D of the 51st Air Rescue
Squadron. (J.B. Chessington)

This rather plain C-124C sits on the ANG ramp at Detroit's Wayne County airport. (W.J. Balogh, Sr.)

Several RF-80As (and RF-86As) were camouflaged during the Korean War, as this 67th TAC Recon Wing shows. (Davis Collection)

Lined up at Hickam AFB, Hawaii are F-84Gs of the 31st Fighter Escort Wing during the FOX PETER ONE mass flight across the Pacific. (BGen. N. Gaddis)

The Continental Division of MATS used their C-97As primarily as freight carriers. (C. Cook)

This F-84E carries the three color markings for the commander of the 58th Fighter Bomber Wing based in Korea. (Colonel J. Ludwig)

This C-54D is seconds away from touchdown at a Korean base with needed supplies. (Major T. Ingrassia)

This 31st Fighter Escort Wing F-84G is bombed up for participation in a training film. (Lt.Colonel J. Meierdierck)

Carrying thirty-two 5' rockets (but not far) for use in a training film, this 31st Fighter Escort Wing F-84G is ready to go. (Lt.Colonel J. Meierdierck)

Yellow trim on this C-82A doesn't help much in disguising her portly lines. (W.T. Larkins)

This C-119B is picking up J-47 engines at a base in Korea for repair at bases in Japan. (I. Clark)

Maintenance personnel make last minute checks to this F-84G of the 27th Fighter Escort Group prior to FOX PETER TWO, the second mass flight across the Pacific. (Colonel D. Maggert)

Lined up and ready for the next leg of FOX PETER TWO, this row of 27th FEW F-84Gs show their 522 FES colors. (Colonel D. Maggert)

Seen at Travis are most of the 27th FEW F-84Gs participating in FOX PETER TWO. (D. Watt)

This taxiing C-46D in Korea is serving for the second time in the Far East. (J. Sullivan)

Some KB-29Ps of Strategic Air Command carried very plain markings as this example shows. (H.W. Rued)

A "boomer's" eye view of air-to-air refueling of a 508th Strategic Fighter Wing F-84G. (Lt.Colonel C. Martinez)

This C-54G is shinier than usual because it was assigned to a four star general. (W.J. Balogh, Sr.)

The very last B-24 on active flying roster in the USAF was this EZB-24M (E meaning exempt, and Z meaning obsolete) from Wright Field. (E.W. Quandt)

Displaying extensive insignia red arctic markings, this 59th FIS F-94B prepares to land at Goose AB, Labrador. (Hanes Collection)

Under rare winter sunshine, a 59th FIS F-94B at Goose AB is filled up with JP-1 fuel. (Hanes Collection)

Every USAF pilot awarded their wings in the early 1950s flew T-6Gs such as this one from Columbus AFB, MS. (Colonel R. Uppstrom)

This SA-16A has landed wheels-up on the snow without any damage. (J.B. Chessington)

With a C-74 support aircraft in background these 31st Fighter Escort Wing F-84Gs undergo en route maintenance in North Africa. (USAF)

In August 1953 the 31st Fighter Escort Wing took part in Operation Longstride with F-84Gs. (USAF)

A factory fresh L-20A awaits a ferry pilot to fly it to base in the "north country." (W.J. Balogh, Sr.)

This Tachikawa AB, Japan based 22nd Troop Carrier Squadron C-124A awaits further work on her #2 engine. (R.B Ochs)

This EF-89B was used at Wright-Patterson AFB as a "chase" aircraft with her gun ports covered. (R.G. Curtis)

The last unit to fly the Twin Mustang was the Alaska based 449th FIS with their insignia red trimmed F-82Hs. (Mr. Spry)

On dispersal at Itazuke AB, Japan an F-86F of the 36th FBS displays her red markings. (C. Martinez)

Since staff cars are lined up, more than likely the passengers on this C-121A, are senior officials of some type. (A. Reuely)

SH-19Bs replaced H-5s for rescue missions in Korea. (R.C. Hyatt)

The markings used by the Military Air Transport Service such as on this C-47D, are about as elaborate as any ever used by the USAF. (W.J. Balogh, Sr.)

The F-84Gs of the Strategic Fighter Wing carried some very sharp markings as can be seen. (Colonel D. Maggert)

Even in the "Jet Age", an old war horse TB-29A is of interest to Open House visitors. (Colonel R. Uppstrom)

Here is a 508th SFW F-84G "plugged into" a KC-97 during the record breaking flight "Operation Longstride." (Colonel D. Maggert)

Three F-84Es of the 406th FBW cruise high over England. (Lt.Colonel F. Smith)

The 363rd TRG painted red checks on all of their assigned aircraft, including this RB-26C. (Colonel R. Uppstrom)

Not all H-19Bs were assigned to rescue units. This one was assigned to support of a bombing and gunnery range. (Colonel R. Johnson)

C-97As were used by MATS as one of their faster transports during the early 1950s. (B. Beecroft)

This C-47D carries the U.S. AIR FORCE lettering on its wings which was used briefly during 1953 on many different types. (USAF)

The yellow trim on this B-29 meant she was a target-tug. (Colonel B. Butcher)

T-34As were all assigned to Air Training Command whose insignia is on the nose. (W.J. Balogh, Sr.)

Three different sets of markings are visible on these T-34As. (J. McCann)

The Gyrfalcon insignia of the 449th FIS was handed and applied to both sides of their F-94A fuselages at Ladd AFB, Alaska. (D. Dickman)

Only one T-34 turboprop powered YC-124B was ever built. (Lt.Colonel W. Duncan)

The Thunderbirds flew the F-84G during their first two years and in doing so, flew their tightest formations. (W.J. Balogh, Sr.)

Some MATS aircraft carried plain markings, such as these carried on a TB-25J. (H. Rued)

This B-17G was an SB-17G at one time, but all of the yellow rescue markings have been removed for other duties. (C.N. Trask)

This F-84F displays three colors on her fin to indicate one of the senior officers of the 405th Fighter Bomber Wing. (R. Warren)

The 1954 Dayton Air Show featured such esoteric aircraft as the X-1A. (W.J. Balogh, Sr.)

This MN ANG F-94A has had its wing tips modified to F-94B standards. (G. Markraf)

The Truax Field, WI based 433rd FIS painted their F-89Cs with this unique design.

Left and below: The 421st Air Refueling Squadron KB-29Ms originally had "rainbow" markings on their noses, wing tips and vertical fins. (USAF)

The third aircraft ordered in fiscal year 1950 was this B-47B based at Edwards AFB, CA. (Lt.Colonel W. Duncan)

This shot is a bit fuzzy, but color shots of the XB-51s are rare, so it is included. (Lt.Colonel W. Duncan)

A very rare visitor to Francis E. Warren AFB, WY in the fall of 1954 was this rare RB-36H of the 28th Strategic Recon Wing. (P.M. Paulsen)

This target-tug F-80C could also "shoot back" if necessary, as can be seen inside the armament compartment with guns and ammo cans. (J. Michaels)

MATS used C-45Gs for proficiency flying and light transport duties. (W.J. Balogh, Sr.)

On the snow covered Chitose AB, Japan ramp, the pilot, his family and his crew chief pose by "their" F-86F of the 334th Fighter Squadron. (Unknown)

For many years, Air Force navigators and bombardiers trained on the T-29C. (W.J. Balogh, Sr.)

This MATS C-124A has not yet received her nose radar installation.

USAF owned and Civil Air Patrol operated L-16s were parked in with privately owned aircraft in those long ago '50s. (H.W. Rued)

This Minn. ANG F-94B towed targets during the all ANG gunnery meet at Gowen Field, ID in the fall of 1954. (R.M. Paulsen)

Left and bottom: The only YKB-29T was assigned to the 421st Refueling Squadron. (Colonel R. Uppstrom)

The Air Force Reserve used T-28As in several units, such as this one from the 349th Fighter Bomber Wing. (H. Rued)

This "Dollar Nineteen" revs up her engines prior to pulling out on the active runway for take-off. (E. Erwin)

One of the F-94Bs the Mass. ANG flew at the 1954 ANG gunnery meet was used to tow targets, hence the extensive orange painted areas. (P.M. Paulsen)

The transport sister of the B-36 bomber, the XC-99 was actually a bit longer but was never lucky enough to have the J-47 jet pods installed. (W.J. Balogh, Sr.)

The crow insignia on the nose of this RB-57A means she was assigned to the 30th TAC Recon Squadron in USAFE. (Major S. Sloan)

The service title and buzz number left no room for the national insignia on this T-34A. (C. Nelson)

This F-94B was one of two modified to carry the M-61 Vulcan rotating barrel cannon later used in the F-104, and wound up in the Mass. ANG as a trainer. (P.M. Paulsen)

This green trimmed C-124A was assigned to the 374th Troop Carrier Wing at Tachikawa AB, Japan.

Some of the markings carried by F-94Cs were very spectacular, as can be seen on this 27th FIS example. (W.J. Balogh, Sr.)

Two orange colored drone director DB-17Ps are framed by a C-47 while transient at Scott AFB, IL. (P.M. Paulsen)

Left and below: The official color to use on target-tug AF/ANG aircraft was orange, but yellow was a good substitute, as this Kentucky ANG F-51D proved. (P.M. Paulsen)

Thule AB, Greenland was one of the many bases used by the KC-97Gs of the 320th Air Refueling Squadron on temporary duty tours. (O'Neal Collection)

The Conn. ANG used this F-84D as a target-tug at the October 1954 ANG gunnery meet. (P.M Paulsen)

The 461st Bomb Wing at Blythville AFB, AR flew B-57s as mission aircraft and this L-20A in a support role. (W.J. Balogh, Sr.)

The AF Reserve's 349th FBW carried very colorful markings on their F-80Cs. (H.W. Rued)

The final production model of the "Flying Box Car" was the C-119G. (Colonel R. Uppstrom)

An unusual view of an unusual (for the time) event: SAC KC-97 refueling a USAFE F-84G of the 77th FBS. (Lt.Colonel R. Satterfield)

High over Mt. Vesuvius, an F-84G of the 77th FBS banks left. (Lt.Colonel R. Satterfield)

The first Fairchild built C-123B taxis by the aviation press at her first public showing. (W.J. Balogh, Sr.)

A refueling crew services this T-28A while its pilot crouches on the wing. (Major B. Gordon)

The unit commander of the North Dakota Air National Guard's fighter squadron was assigned this F-94C. (via D. Slowiak)

The largest lifeboats ever carried by an aircraft were the ones SB-29s carried. (USAF)

The Alaska ANG's 144th FBS flew their F-80Cs down to Boise, ID for the ANG gunnery meet. (P.M. Paulsen)

The radar nose on MATS AC-47Ds did little to improve the looks of the aircraft. (H. Ruad)

Three red stripes around fuselage on this 46th FIS indicate the squadron commander's aircraft. (O'Donnell via Ethell)

SAC aircraft were not really noted for elaborate markings, and this KC-97G is no exception. (W.J. Balogh, Sr.)

The 405th FBW flew F-84Fs out of Langley AFB, VA. (Lt.Colonel R. Satterfield)

Several B-47Bs were used for various test programs at Edwards AFB, CA such as this one. (W. Duncan)

The only thing unusual about this rather plain B-25J is the two sets of buzz numbers painted on it. (Colonel R. Uppstrom)

This is the F-80C the Texas ANG used to tow targets at the all-ANG gunnery meet in October 1954. (P.M. Paulsen)

The 1954 all ANG gunnery meet at Gowen Field, Idaho in October was the Mustang's swan song at such events. (P.M. Paulsen)

One of the more colorful unit markings used by the Air Force Reserve were those used by the T-33As of the 349th Fighter Bomber Wing. (H.W. Rued)

The $100,000 MiG-15 sits on the Patterson AFB, OH ramp between test flights. (R.G. Curtiss)

Overall red with white upper wing surfaces and markings, such as on these two QB-17Ns, were the mid-1950s scheme for drone target aircraft. (via Colonel J. Morris)

This B-25J with complete MATS markings was photographed at the old National Guard area at Chicago's Midway Airport.

The Keystone state was repre-
sented by this F-84F at the 1955
Ricks Race from Los Angeles to
Detroit.

This L-16A was assigned to a
Civil Air Patrol unit at a dirt
strip airport that is now
beneath condos in the author's
home town.

These SA-16As were assigned to
the 58th Air Rescue Squadron at
Wheelus AB, Libya. (C. Cook)

This brand new RB-52B has just arrived at Patterson Field, Ohio from the factory for extensive testing. (R.G. Curtiss)

The 1700th Air Transport Group (test) at Kelly AFB, TX flew turbo-prop versions of the Stratofreighter with the designation YC-97J. (Mr. Fagen)

Cruising over the clouds is a C-47D of the Air Training Command. (USAF)

This Thule based 74th IS F-89C collapsed its nose gear and is awaiting repairs. (O'Neal Collection)

The only known VB-29 was assigned to Guam sporting an almost airliner paint scheme.

The 74th FIS flew F-89Cs out of "sunny" Thule AB, Greenland. (J. Ford)

With JATO bottles attached to her sides, this SA-16A is ready to taxi out for a demonstration of a jet assisted take-off. (W.J. Balogh, Sr.)

The rainbow markings on the fin of this KB-29M meant she was assigned to the 421st Air Refueling Squadron in Japan. (J. Hilliard)

This Selfridge based SH-19A hovers while awaiting ATC clearance to depart Detroit's Wayne County airport. (W.J. Balogh, Sr.)

TAC aircraft visible include F-100As of 479th FDW, F-84Fs of 401st FBW, and RB-57As of 363rd TRW. (Mr. Brown)

This Ore. ANG F-94B has just intercepted a B-36D and is then flying formation with it. (Lt.Colonel C. Toynbee)

One of the two squadrons in PACAF to fly the RF-84F was the 15th Recon Squadron at Kadena AB, Okinawa. (Colonel B. Mathews)

T-6Gs were used for training and proficiency flying well into the 1950s. (Lt.Colonel A. Bruder)

Pale blue is an unusual color for unit markings, but the 321st FIS decided to be different and use it. (J. Ford)

Air Material Command used many C-47Ds as personnel transports. (W.J. Balogh, Sr.)

The 354th FIS F-94Cs originally carried subdued markings. (M. McCann)

This gaggle of T-6Gs was parked at a US air base in England prior to delivery to the new post-WWII German Luftwaffe. (D. Callahan)

The pilot and crew chief of this F-86L of the 94th FIS, 30th Air Division from Selfridge confer just before the aircraft starts to taxi out. (Lt.Colonel A. Bruder)

High over Mt. St. Helens, an anonymous F-94C cruises in the sunshine. (C. Dickman)

The commander of the Alaskan Air Command was assigned this C-54D which displayed the Big Dipper insignia on its nose. (USAF)

Many a transient T-6G passed through the ILL. ANG facility that was in the southwest corner of Chicago's Midway Airport.

During the summer of 1955, an F-89D was towed to Chicago's lakefront to participate in General Motor's "Powerarama" show. (W. Kaepplinger)

The MINN ANG marked their F-51Ds in a very classy style. (MINN ANG)

The seagull insignia on the nose of this F-94B means she is assigned to the 101st FIS of the MASS ANG. (P.M. Paulsen)

The Airways and Air Communications Service division of MATS used this C-45G as a personnel transport. (W.J. Balogh, Sr.)

The "Lightning Lancers" of the 68th FIS flew F-94Bs at Itazuke AB, Japan such as this one. (C.F. Toler)

With her landing gear almost completely retracted, this T-33A heads out for another training sortie. (Lt.Colonel A. Bruder)

Right and below: This 42nd Bomb Wing B-36D prepares to depart the Detroit Air Show in early July 1955.

Matador "pilotless bombers" were assigned to several locations in Germany, such as this display example at Hahn. (Colonel R. Johnson)

The 12th Strategic Fighter Wing commander flew this three color trimmed F-84F. (E.W. Lippincott)

B-17Gs served well into the 1950s, such as this drone director DB-17G. (Colonel R.E. Clark)

Originally, the 48th FBW carried very simple markings on her Huns. (G. Kennell)

The first F-102A squadron in the AF was the 327th FIS at George AFB. (J. Michaels)

This Edwards B-45A carries arctic markings for duty in the snow country. (W. Duncan)

The Test Pilot School at Edwards AFB used this F-84E in its curriculum.

Six turning and four burning! An RB-36F cruises at high altitude somewhere over the United States.

Republic built two turboprop versions of the F-84, designated XF-84H, and to some people, that was two too many. (Lt.Colonel W. Duncan)

With tires smoking, this 388th FBW F-100D lands at Etain following a training sortie, still carrying insignia red arctic markings. (F. Street)

While displaying her huge wing area, this 57th Fighter Interceptor Wing F-89D also shows where the insignia red arctic markings were painted. (USAF)

Chanute AFB, IL maintained a fleet of T-28As such as this one so pilots attending technical courses could maintain their proficiency. (Colonel R.E. Clark)

This Edwards AFB F-89D is being used to test fire Falcon & Genie missiles so carries extensive gloss white and red fluorescent areas on it. (USAF)

Right and below: This F-101A was the one flown to Ladd AFB for cold weather tests. One view shows her landing back in Ohio, w/chute while the other was taken at below zero temperature at Ladd. (R. Parmeter) (Mr. Freeman)

This F-102A was flown at Ladd AFB for cold weather tests. (Mr. Freeman)

On a sleepy summer day, this Clovis AFB, NM based L-20A cruises over the arid fields of New Mexico. (R.B. Ochs)

High over northern Japan this 8th FBS F-84G shows refueling probes installed in her tip tanks. (Unknown)

Here is another view of 194 showing tip tank probes in use. (Unknown)

The markings of 354th FIS F-94Cs were similar to those used by the 8th FBW in Korea. (USAF)

Open house days at Edwards AFB in the 1950s often meant static displays of such aircraft as this X-1. (W. Duncan)

Another Air Force experimental aircraft on display at Edwards was the one and only X-3. (W. Duncan)

The X-5 was one of the pioneers of variable-sweep wing technology. (W. Duncan)

A rare bird indeed! One of the P2V-7s obtained from the Navy for still highly classified missions as the RB-69A. (S.H. Miller)

The snow was blowing when this 55th Strategic Recon Wing RB-47H was photographed at Thule AB, Greenland. (O'Neal Collection)

An early production F-102A is displayed at an Edwards AFB open house. (W. Duncan)

Why this A-26B got two sets of buzz numbers is still anyone's guess. (Lt.Colonel E. Bosetti)

High speed target towing in the mid-1950s was performed by TB-45As such as this one. (B. Hostetter)

An emergency landing on a beach was serious enough that this C-119F was scrapped (Colonel J.J. Tarsitano)

A rare sight at Williams AFB, AZ was this B-47B of the 320th Bomb Wing. (Lt.Colonel E. Bosetti)

The original markings on 327th FIS F-102As were rather subdued. (USAF)

When later model F-102As were received by the 327th FIS, the markings became much more elaborate. (J. McCann)

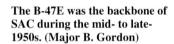

The B-47E was the backbone of SAC during the mid- to late-1950s. (Major B. Gordon)

This KB-29P carries the markings of the 420th Air Refueling based at RAF Sculthorpe in England. (MSGT. D.B. Hyde)

The flight crew of this 449th FIS F-89D is discussing possible write-ups after their just completed flight. (R. Preciado)

The 4th Tow Target Squadron from George AFB, CA would fly their TB-26Cs up to Ladd AFB on temporary duty pulling targets for Army AAA gunners.

The Fifth Air Force in Japan also had a tow target squadron assigned that flew B-26s. (J. Snelson)

The overall insignia red color used to identify drone aircraft gave way to fluorescents in the late-1950s, such as on this QF-80B. (C. Nelson)

This C-54D based at Tachikawa AB, Japan was used as a medical evacuation aircraft. (R. Johnson)

The countdown for the launch of this air-breathing Matador missile from a range in North Africa has begun, and personnel are hurrying to safety. (Lt.Colonel J. Pool)

Major A. Drew set a new speed record in this F-101A. (USAF)

The Tactical Air Command was the primary user of the C-123B during the 1950s and early 1960s. (H. Rued)

Flaring for a landing at Otis AFB, MA is an RC-121C of the Air Defense Command. (P. Paulsen)

Green for a squadron color is unusual, but the 437th FIS used it well on their F-89Ds. (H. Morgan)

Far East Air Force F-84Gs had to refuel behind KB-29s with a tip tank mounted probe into the tanker's "basket." (USAF)

Even in Alaska, it did not take the sun long to start fading the insignia red markings on this 433rd Fighter Interceptor Squadron F-89D at Ladd AFB.

This B-50A was based at Logan airport Boston to participate in electronic equipment testing. (P. Paulsen)

The double diagonal fin stripes on the B-47B meant she was assigned to the 320th Bomb Wing. (BGen. K.W. Bell)

The latter part of the B-29's career saw them used for towing targets. (USAF)

The RB-45Cs of the 19th TAC Recon Squadron were all assigned to England where this one is on display. (D.B. Hyde)

Red tail and wing tips on this C-54E indicate duty in northern climes. (H. Rued)

The Glasgow AFB, MT area had enough snow around it that 29th FIS F-94Cs carried insignia red arctic markings. (C. Nelson)

Two 41st FIS F-86Ds break right "somewhere over Japan." (USAF)

This plain-jane F-102A was used by Air Research and Development Command. (C. Stewart)

This H-21B is en route to duty in snow country so is painted with insignia red arctic markings. (W.J. Balogh, Sr.)

One of two PACAF units to fly the RF-84F was the 45th TAC Recon Squadron at Misawa AB, Japan. (Lt.Colonel C. Martinez)

Even chilly weather didn't keep spectators away from an open house static display of a KC-97G. (A.W. George)

A visiting F-102A draws curious Guardsmen at Logan airport. (P.M. Paulsen)

This 39th FIS F-86D's afterburner blasts the night during a ground run-up. (USAF)

This formation is made up of 445th FIS F-89Ds participating in a fly-by over Detroit. (A.J. Miller)

MATS C-124As supported the many TAC deployments such as this one at Cannon AFB, NM. (D. Henderson)

Right and below: Two views of the F-102A bailed to General Electric to test their J85 that is slung under the fuselage.

The 47th Bomb Wing flew B-66Bs after B-45s were retired. (D.B. Hyde)

The 47th Bomb Wing flew B-45As in Europe from 1952-1958. (T. Cress)

This three-ship formation is from the 4th Fighter Wing Day. (Colonel D. Elmer)

The 58th Air Rescue Squadron eventually traded in their SA-16As for the improved SA-16B. (T. Cress)

The 83rd Fighter Interceptor Squadron F-104As were sent TDY to bases on Taiwan during the 1958 Quemoy Crisis. (USAF)

The absence of tail guns and the large number painted on the fin means this B-47B was assigned to the 4347th Combat Crew Training Wing of SAC. (J. McCann)

The only C model Huns based in Europe belonged to the 36th FDW at Bitburg AB, Germany. (T. Cress)

The 479th FBW was the first AF combat unit equipped with F-100s in 1954, and later traded A models for Cs such as this one. (Colonel A. Johnson)

MATS used AC-47Ds as airways and landing aids inspection aircraft such as this example. (W.J. Balogh, Sr.)

Shaw AFB, SC was the home base of the 432nd TAC Recon Group and their RF-101Cs. (Colonel A. Johnson)

The PA ANG also used yellow paint for target tugs, as on this T-33A. (C. Stewart)

The 463rd Troop Carrier Wing painted their C-130As in an eye-catching scheme. (R. Parmerter)

Three pilots of the 8th TFW swap notes after landing at Itazuke AB, Japan. (Colonel W. Davis)

It is easy to see how the nickname "Blue Canoe" was applied to the Cessna built L-27As. (W.J. Balogh, Sr.)

A KB-50 is in position for two 506th FBW Huns to "plug in" for some fuel. (C. Nichols)

This RF-101A was flown by the commander of the 363rd TAC Recon Wing which was composed of the 363rd and 432nd TAC Recon Groups. (McDonnell Aircraft)

When MATS completed their testing of one YC-97J, it was transferred to Norton AFB, CA for use as an executive transport. (J. Michaels Collection)

The extensive fluorescent orange paint on this F-101B indicates she is involved in some kind of test program. (Colonel C.W. King)

This B-57E is being "checked out" by airmen at Clovis AFB, NM. (D. Henderson)

Helio's very first Courier for the USAF was this L-28A finished in a sinister overall gloss black. (P. Paulsen)

An Open House at Edwards AFB included the fifth production F-101B. (Lt.Colonel W. Duncan)

This Wright Air Development Center F-105B carries arctic markings to participate in cold weather tests at Ladd AFB, AK. (D. Ostrowski)

The 31st FBW really gussied up
her gunnery meet entrants.
(Colonel W. Johnson)

The MICH ANG RF-84Fs were
among the shiniest in the
inventory. (W.J. Balogh, Sr.)

When the 15th TRS traded in
RF-84Fs for RF-101Cs, the same
markings were carried. (Colonel
B. Mathews)

When the conspicuous markings craze hit the USAF in the late 1950s, the SA-16Bs of the Air Rescue Service were not exempt. (T. Cress)

By the time the 449th FIS at Ladd AFB, Alaska transitioned from F-89Ds to F-89Js, they were the last Scorpion unit in the state.

USAFE used three types of recon configured bombers, and this rare shot caught two of them, and RB-57A and RB-66B. (T. Cress)

The 388th FBW markings remained after the unit was renumbered 49th in December 1957. (T. Cress)

F-102As normally based at Elmendorf AFB are caught at Ladd AFB after a cross-country flight. (R.A. Diozzi)

The only USAFE unit to fly the RF-101C was the 66th TAC Recon Wing based at several bases in France. (Lt.Colonel K. Hemphill)

This production F-105B was used for extensive air-to-air refueling tests. (Major E. Sommerich)

The shortest runway ever! This Hun survived 16 zero length take-offs from this trailer and later served with several ANG units. (Colonel D. Elmer)

Tyndall AFB, FL used H-21Bs to retrieve Q-2 drone targets. (Lt. Colonel A. Bruder)

The 363rd TAC REcon Group was one of the two groups based at Shaw AFB with RF-101Cs. (D. Ostrowski)

This B-47E is taxiing out for take-off from an Alaskan base. (R. Diozzi)

The 474th FBW has displayed herring bone markings on almost every model jet fighter flown since 1951 as this F-100F shows. (D. Henderson)

The SD ANG used this TB-25K to train their radar officers for the unit's F-89s. (P. Paulsen)

When the 322nd Air Division was based in France in the early 1960s, it was equipped with C-130As. (T. Richeson)

This F-100F was Colonel Francis Gabreski's mount when he was commander of the 354th TFW. (T. Cress)

The only B-57 equipped Bomb Wing assigned to USAFE was the 38th at Laon AB, France with B-57Bs. (Lt.Colonel K. Hemphill)

This MATS C-124A feathered her number 1 and number 4 propellers for reasons unknown. (D. Henderson)

These 79th TFS Huns bask in the bright Wheelus AB sun. (T. Cress)

Nestled in with sister B-50s of various models is a rare version, a KB-50K. (J. Michaels)

Two JF-105Bs were tested with camera noses, and 112 was one of them. (Major E. Sommerich)

Sporting insignia red arctic markings for her ferry flight to the 50th TFW in France, 041 receives last minute checks prior to take-off. (MSGT. M. Olmsted)

The very first C-133A went on
to serve with MATS after
extensive testing at Edwards.
(D.B. Hyde)

This Hun belongs to the
commander of the 36th Fighter
Day Wing and displays the five
colors of the assigned squadrons. (T. Cress)

The yellow bands on this RB-
66B indicate assignment to the
30th TAC Recon Squadron. (T.
Cress)

Left and below: A 31st TFW Hun is shown approaching and then plugging in to the refueling basket of a KB-50. (Lt.Colonel T. Barnes)

This 50th TFW F-100D was transferred to the Danish Air Force late in 1960.

The late 1950s saw the beginning of conspicuous fluorescent orange markings such as on the C-47D.

The 49th TFW used this three color style of markings beginning in 1960.

The Wright Air Development Center used this NT-33A that has been fitted with an RT-33A nose for various electronic tests. (Major E.M. Sommerich)

Another famous AF unit insignia graces the tail of this F-106A of the 94th FIS. (W.J. Balogh, Sr.)

The flight line steam plant at Misawa AB Japan forms the background for this 21st TAC Fighter Wing F-100D. (R. Keister)

The USAFE KB-50J equipped Air Refueling Squadron was the 420th based at RAF Sculthorpe in England.

This view from the port refueling position of a KB-50 shows a 27th TFW F-100D. (Lt.Colonel R. Elam)

This 8th TFW F-100F takes on fuel from a 421st Air Refueling Squadron KB-50. (USAF)

When SAC phased out their RF-84Ks, the MICH ANG at Detroit's Wayne County Airport received several. (W.J. Balogh, Sr.)

Some Tactical Air Command C-130As were painted with fluorescent orange arctic markings for a brief period.

With a MN-1 practice bomb dispenser under her left wing, this 20th TFW F-100D blasts off the Wheelus runway. (Lt.Colonel T. Barnes)

The third YT-38A was based at Edwards for its service testing. (W. Duncan)

The F-102As of the 326th FIS Richards-Gebaur AFB, MO (Dicky-Goober to the troops) carried these distinctive markings. (T. Love)

The X-15A and its mother ship, the NB-52A, were on display at Edwards in May 1960. (Lt.Colonel W. Duncan)

This F-105B was retained by Republic to test various modifications. (Lt.Colonel R. Satterfield)

The third production F-102A was flown by the 16th FIS on Okinawa. (Colonel A. Picarillo)

The 479th Tactical Fighter Wing's F-104Cs visited many USAFE bases during their many TDY's to Europe in the early 1960s, such as this one at Hahn. (T. Richeson)

This Randolph AFB, TX based T-38A's landing gear is just starting to retract after take-off. (USAF)

The "Dumbo" insignia on the nose means this C-124C belongs to the 19th Logistics Support Squadron out of Kelly AFB, TX. (C. Stewart)

The 11th FIS was based at Duluth, MN with F-102As. This one was assigned to the squadron commander. (SMSGT. N. Weeks)

This gaggle of T-33As is forming up for a formation fly-past over a graduation ceremony. (Major B. Gordon)

Republic Aviation maintained several F-84Fs as test aircraft, as evidenced by all of the non-standard, high-visibility markings painted on this one. (Lt.Colonel R. Satterfield)

The pilot is waving at the crowd as this B-58A taxis at Edwards AFB.

The Tachikawa, Japan based 1503rd Air Transport Wing was the only C-124A unit in the Far East. (B. Mathews)

Sporting purple trim, this 510th TFS F-100D sits on the ramp at Clark AFB. (via G. Geer)

The bombardier nose of this drone-director EDB-26C has been replaced with a solid nose from a B-26B so electronic equipment can be installed. (Major E. Sommerlich)

The 332nd FIS flew the F-102A at Thule AB, Greenland after their tour at England AFB, LA. (MSGT. M. Cross)

The T-39As assigned to Scott AFB, IL received a unique blue paint scheme.

This early 1960s Open House displayed a B-52G with Hound Dog missiles mounted under its wings. (Colonel J.J. Tarsitano)

B-57Es were built from the ground up as high-speed target-tugs, replacing the worn out B-26s, B-29s, and B-45s. (MSGT. Petty)

No, the Army did not equip one of their units with F-89Ds, this was just used to air launch target missiles. (B. Knowles)

The PACAF decal on this KB-50J identifies it as belonging to the 421st Air Refueling Squadron out of Yokota AB, Japan. (E. Van Houten)

Two B-57Bs were modified to accept the guidance system noses of the TM-76 "MACE" tactical missiles and were based in Europe as NB-57Bs.

The only Boundary Layer Control "Herky-bird" was this NC-130B based at Wright Field. (Major E. Sommerlich)

Right and below: St. Louis is home to the 110th Tactical Fighter Squadron who flew the F-84F during the early 1960s. (USAF)

As tensions eased after the 1961 Berlin Crisis, many ANG F-104As were statically displayed at various open houses at USAFE bases. (C. Snyder)

Also from the publisher

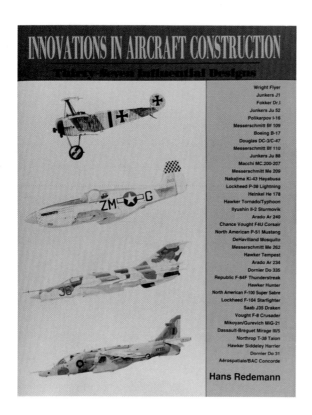

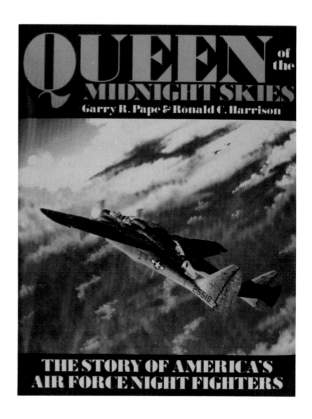

INNOVATIONS IN AIRCRAFT CONSTRUCTION
Thirty-Seven Influential Designs
Hans Redemann

Presented in chronological order are thirty-seven classic designs that changed the history of flight: The Wright Flyer, Junkers J1, Fokker Dr.1, Junkers Ju 52, Polikarpov I-16, Messerschmitt Bf 109, Boeing B-17, Douglas DC-3/C-47, Messerschmitt Bf 110, Junkers Ju 88, Macchi MC.200-207, Messerschmitt Me 209, Nakajima Ki-43 Hayabusa, Lockheed P-38 Lightning, Heinkel He 178, Hawker Tornado/Typhoon, Ilyushin Il-2 Sturmovik, Arado Ar 240, Chance Vought F4U Corsair, North American P-51 Mustang, DeHavilland Mosquito, Messerschmitt Me 262, Hawker Tempest, Arado Ar 234, Dornier Do 335, Republic F-84F Thunderstreak, Hawker Hunter, North American F-100 Super Sabre, Lockheed F-104 Starfighter, Saab J35 Draken, Vought F-8 Crusader, Mikoyan/Gurevich MiG-21, Dassault-Breguet Mirage III/5, Northrop T-38 Talon, Hawker Siddeley Harrier, Dornier Do 31, Aérospatiale/BAC Concorde.

Each aircraft is shown in photographs, scale line drawings from various perspectives, and presents the various models, prototypes and export models, technical aspects and measurements.

Size: 8 1/2" x 11"   248 pages, over 300 photographs, 16 color photographs
ISBN: 0-88740-338-7   hard cover $29.95

QUEEN OF THE MIDNIGHT SKIES
The Story of America's Air Force Night Fighters
Garry R. Pape & Ronald C. Harrison

After twenty years of study and research, Garry Pape and Ronald Harrison's new book chronicles the epic story of the US night fighter program of World War II. Historical accounts of American night fighter pilots, with many first hand accounts of aerial combat over the South Pacific and Europe, as well as the complete history of all night fighter squadrons formed during World War II. Also included is the development of radar and modern air defenses, making this book one of the most detailed on night fighters in World War II.

Complemeting the detailed text are over 650 color and black and white photographs from many sources, including the National Archives, Northrop Aircraft archives, the U.S. Air Force Museum, the Air Force Archives, the Smithsonian Air & Space Museum, and personal interviews with test pilots, designers and engineers.

Size: 8 1/2" x 11"   368 pages, over 650 photographs, 32 color pages, maps
ISBN: 0-88740-415-4   hard cover $45.00

WALKING II
THE SHOES
OF ANOTHE